C000151423

1 MONTH OF
FREE
READING

at
www.ForgottenBooks.com

By purchasing this book you are
eligible for one month membership to
ForgottenBooks.com, giving you
unlimited access to our entire
collection of over 1,000,000 titles via
our web site and mobile apps.

To claim your free month visit:
www.forgottenbooks.com/free166998

* Offer is valid for 45 days from date of purchase. Terms and conditions apply.

ISBN 978-0-428-19117-7
PIBN 10166998

This book is a reproduction of an important historical work. Forgotten Books uses
state-of-the-art technology to digitally reconstruct the work, preserving the original format
whilst repairing imperfections present in the aged copy. In rare cases, an imperfection in
the original, such as a blemish or missing page, may be replicated in our edition. We do,
however, repair the vast majority of imperfections successfully; any imperfections that
remain are intentionally left to preserve the state of such historical works.

Forgotten Books is a registered trademark of FB &c Ltd.
Copyright © 2018 FB &c Ltd.
FB &c Ltd, Dalton House, 60 Windsor Avenue, London, SW19 2RR.
Company number 08720141. Registered in England and Wales.

For support please visit www.forgottenbooks.com

BOARD OF EDUCATION
NILES, OHIO

BULLETIN 1922

The School Housing Problem of Niles, Ohio

Report of a Survey made on request of the
Board of Education

By

GEORGE R. TWISS

Professor of the Principles and Practices of Education
College of Education, The Ohio State University

Niles, Ohio
Printing Dept., McKinley High School
1922

133623 UNIVERSITY of CALIFOR

LOS ANGELES
LIBRARY

CONTENTS

The School Housing Problem

REPORT OF A SURVEY

LETTER OF TRANSMITTAL BY THE SUPERINTENDENT OF SCHOOLS

Niles, Ohio, April 1, 1922.

Mr. F. C. Wagstaff,
    President Board of Education,
        Niles, Ohio.

My dear Sir:

On February 7, 1921, Professor George R. Twiss of the Ohio State University, was requested to make a survey of the present housing facilities of the Niles Public Schools and make recommendations for a building program. Professor Twiss spent about five days in Niles, during which time he visited every school several times in addition to visiting every part of the city. The superintendent of schools and teachers collected a great mass of materials, statistics, blue prints and carefully marked maps. These materials were placed in the hands of Professor. Twiss, who spent more than ten days in working over the materials of his own observations and the materials supplied by others.

I have the honor of transmitting the completed report to the Board of Education. The work of the specialist was very carefully done. The figures are accurate; estimates for the future are conservative. I commend the report to the Board of Education and the citizens of the Niles City School District for careful perusal and thou·htful study. I believe it points the way which will lead to continued conservative progress.

Very respectfully,

(Signed) S. L. EBY,
    Superintendent of Schools.

INTRODUCTION BY THE PRESIDENT OF THE BOARD OF EDUCATION

The Board of Education of the Niles City School District has been laboring under two handicaps since the beginning of the Great War, namely, lack of revenue and lack of school buildings. It has been necessary to levy taxes to the limit permitted by law, but even by so doing the Niles City Board of Education has up to the present time been unable to keep pace with the rapidly growing school system in Niles. The Board of Education has given unstintingly almost unlimited time, its best thought, and conscientious labor. The Board secured the services of Professor Twiss, who served on the staff which made a survey of the schools of Wilmington, Delaware. He was also a member of the commission sent under the auspices of the United States Bureau of Education to make a survey of the schools of the Hawaiian Islands. Since making the survey in Niles, Professor Twiss was commissioned by the General Education Board to make a survey of the colored secondary schools and colleges in the South.

The report which follows has been held in abeyance until the present time. In some ways this has been an advantage. The statistics are those of the school year 1921. Experience for the year 1922 has proved unexpected accuracy in predictions of enrolment. In fact, figures of the report tend to fall below rather than surpass actual figures of enrolment in the next three or four years. This fact proves the wisdom of the Board of Education in securing an expert to make the present study and furthermore demonstrates the necessity of placing the information in the report in the hands of interested citizens in order that there may be no delay in making adequate provisions for the upper grades of our schools.

Since the first draft of the report was submitted a number of the recommendations pertaining to the elementary schools have been carried out. The recommendations which touch the Junior and Senior High Schools are matters for the future.

The Board of Education submit the text of the report to the public for careful study and constructive criticism. The schools are yours, the moneys to be expended are yours. The members of the Board are your conscientious servants. They solicit your support in carrying out either in whole or in part the recommendations of the following report. Action is imperative; delay is folly.

(Signed) FRANK C. WAGSTAFF,
President Niles City Board of Education.

REASONS FOR THE SURVEY

The City of Niles has been growing very rapidly. Within the space of a few years the school system has developed from a village system to a city school system. The school system has not kept pace with the growth and development of the city. The restrictions of war times have aggravated the inadequacy of buildings and funds for school purposes.

Another factor which contributed largely in rendering the school facilities of Niles inadequate is the great emphasis laid on high school and college training in the army. The preference shown in the army for men of higher education has given a strong incentive to young men to get at least a high school education in order not to be handicapped in the future. The struggle for a higher education has tended to fill the upper grades in all public schools.

A third factor contributing to the congestion of the upper grades of our school system is the change in the compulsory education laws. The latest law requires all youth to remain in school until the age of 16, and through the seventh grade. The normal child will have had two years of high school work and the retarded pupil at least one year of junior high school work. Under the old law the age limit was one year lower.

A glance at maps showing the geographic distribution of the pupils in the Niles schools shows that about two-thirds of the pupils live in the east end of the city. At present there are buildings with sixty-six school rooms west of Mosquito Creek where one-third of the pupils live. East of the creek to accommodate two-thirds of the pupils there are twenty-eight rooms. The distribution of buildings no longer conforms to the distribution of school population. For the reason of the present distribution of school buildings it is important to have a survey in order that there may be a readjustment of buildings to school population.

The last decade has seen notable advances in public school administration. Progressive boards of education are employing the same principles of business and scientific management that private business is using. Boards of education no longer are pursuing a narrow policy, but have a vision of future growth and needs. They are formulating policies which look twenty, thirty, forty and even fifty years in the future. Careful study of past and present conditions and needs will give reasonable certainty in predicting future conditions and needs. In no field of public service is insight and vision more important than in public education.

The Niles City Board of Education has had thrust upon them a keen realization of rapid growth of the city, the increasing importance attached to the higher phases of education, the increased responsibility thrust upon the public schools by the new compulsory education laws, the increasing maladjustment of school buildings to school population. Realizing the foregoing, having a vision of and a faith in the future of Niles, and having adopted sound principles of scientific business management, the Board of Education has not only given most careful thought to the problems confronting them, but has called upon the specialist for his counsel and recommendations. The Board of Education, the Superintendent of Schools and the specialist have pooled their efforts and best thoughts. This is at least partially crystallized and reduced to permanent form in the following report. By a careful study and constructive criticism there will be formulated a composite judgment which will guide in giving Niles a progressive, economical and adequate school system. The following report is commended to all friends of education in the City of Niles for their study, for criticism, for additional suggestions.

AN APPEAL TO THE PUBLIC FOR SUPPORT
AND CO-OPERATION

The Niles City Board of Education has been making a conscientious effort to provide the city of Niles with a system of schools second to none in the state. The responsibility has been heavy and the difficulties great. Efforts have been directed along the line of scientific management in the administration of the schools; of formulating a course of study adapted to the needs of the community; of furnishing the best possible instruction; and providing adequate facilities, such as school buildings and equipment in order that the educational work may be carried on as it should be.

The chief difficulty in carrying out the educational policy of the Board of Education has been lack of school rooms and equipment. To date the provisions for the first six grades are almost adequate to give all the children a seat all day in a regular school room.

The upper grades are at present most seriously handicapped. Next year the senior high school will be more than double what it was in 1915. By 1924 the senior high school will enroll 800 at a conservative estimate. The junior high school enrolls 438 at present. This department will increase. By 1925 these two departments will have an enrollment of 1300 to 1400 students. Present high school accommodations provide for not more than 600 to 650 if state laws and rules of hygiene and sanitation are obeyed. The Board of Education has permission to use Old Central only through the year 1922-1923. What is to be done after 1923 is problematical. It is a fact that room must be found somewhere for 600 to 800 high school students by September 1924. Conditions at best will be unsatisfactory next year. Every year will be worse until sufficient room will be provided for the junior and senior high schools.

Niles is growing rapidly. Enrolment has increased the past few years at the rate of 260 a year. This means six to eight rooms and teachers a year must be added. Every year a building of at least six rooms must be built to take care of increased enrolment. There is only one condition which will render the school plant in Niles adequate, namely, a complete arrest in the growth and prosperity of Niles. No one having faith in our city can believe such a condition possible. It is more reasonable to believe that 1922 will witness 250 new pupils entering the Niles schools—one six-room building; 1923, 250 pupils—another six-room building; 1924, 250 pupils, still another six-room building. As soon as it can be built the Niles schools will fill a new sixteen-room building. The new building should be one adaptable to elementary school, junior high school and senior high school work. The building should have facilities for teaching a varied course of study. As soon as it could be built it would probably have assigned to it elementary pupils and junior high school pupils. There is a probability that within a few years it would have to take care of several hundred senior high school pupils.

The Board of Education is the representative body of the citizens of Niles, whose duty it is to provide facilities for the education of the children of Niles. In certain respects the Board of Education can take no action without the direct approval of the electors of the school district. Any expenditure of money other than for current operating expense requires the direct approval of the electors. There are a few exceptions to this general statement. Howver, any project such as suggested in this report will require a majority vote of the electors. Every citizen of Niles should keep in mind the one great outstanding fact, THE INCREASE IN ENROLMENT IN THE NILES SCHOOLS IS 260 PER YEAR, EVERY YEAR REQUIRES THE ADDITION OF SIX TO EIGHT SCHOOL ROOMS TO TAKE CARE OF THE INCREASE. To build one small building each year would be impractical. The only feasible solution of the problem confronting the Board of Education is to build school houses in much larger units than in the past. By so doing it will be wise economy in all respects. The citizens of Niles are most urgently invited to study the growth of the Niles schools as set forth in this report. Their support and co-operation is most important in solving the problem confronting Niles. Superintendents and boards of education are the servants of the public. They come and go. The schools belong to the people and are as permanent as the city itself. The future welfare and prosperity of Niles depends to a great degree on her public schools. Every citizen who is interested in the progress and prosperity of our city should use his influence towards providing adequate facilities for the school children of Niles. The responsibility is yours, the Board of Education are your servants. They are awaiting your decision on the next step to be taken in providing sufficient school buildings to take care of the upper grades of the public schools. What will your decision be?

CHAPTER I.

THE CITY AND THE PROBLEM

I. THE CITY, PRESENT AND FUTURE.

Niles is pre-eminently a manufacturing city. Situated as it is, in the Mahoning Valley, strategically placed by nature at a convenient meeting point for the iron ore from the upper lake region, and the coal and coke from the Pennsylvania and Ohio fields, in close proximity to the limestone and fireclay deposits needed for fluxes and furnace linings, and with abundant outlying territory over which it may expand, the destiny of the city as a large manufacturing center for iron and steel products is clearly indicated. To these natural advantages are added the transportation facilities afforded by three railways, the Erie, the Pennsylvania and the Baltimore & Ohio, and the P. & O. interurban trolley line. To these, it is pointed out, may be added in the not distant future, the long dreamed-of ship canal from Lake Erie to the Ohio River.

In view of these facts and indications, it is confidently predicted by business men that before many years have rolled by the entire Mahoning Valley between Warren and Youngstown will have become one continuous manufacturing community.

Niles is already growing rapidly. According to the United States census of 1910, its population was 8,361. The 1920 census reports it as 13,080. This is an increase for the ten-year period of 4,719, or 56 per cent.

With the growth of the city in population and wealth, there has come to its people a rising consciousness of resourcefulness and power, and a pride of enterprise and public spirit which gives promise that her people are ready to grapple with their problems of public interest in a forward-looking way. They are beginning to think time not in months and years, but in decades, and to estimate costs not in hundreds of dollars, but in hundreds of thousands.

II. FACTORS OF THE SCHOOL BUILDING PROBLEM.

Absolutely the most important factor in the future growth and prosperity of the city is the education of her citizens. The knowledge, the training, the enterprising spirit of the men and women who are now directing the city's destinies must be passed on to the rising generation of children, who will soon be controlling the activities in which their parents are now engaged. If **education is not provided** for in the best and most scientific manner, the city will fall behind other and neighboring communities both in material prosperity, and in all those spiritual qualities that make a city an advantageous place in which to live and work. Hence in any large and forward-looking program for city development,—in any plans for the future which may be shaping themselves in the minds of the members of the Chamber of Commerce, Rotary Club, Kiwanis Club, Federation of Churches, Women's Clubs or other organizations commonly taking part in city development—the schools and their needs must be among the first and most important items to receive consideration.

Shall Niles pursue a hand-to-mouth policy, resorting year after year to such expedients as crowding children into school rooms beyond their normal seating capacity and air space, or as placing them in ill-lighted and ill-ventilated basement rooms? Shall she remand her children to condemned and abandoned buildings, or place them in portables, which obstruct the light and occupy the playground space, or restrict them to the unpopular and inefficient platoon system with half-day sessions? With an average new crop of nearly three hundred children coming on each year, and with the high school building now crowded to forty per cent beyond its normal capacity, shall the board of education delay until three or four hundred children are turned out on the streets before it plans a new building or even secures a site for one? This is the way that the school building problem has been handled in hundreds of our growing cities during the past fifty years; and it has resulted in enormous and pitiable economic and social wastes.

Fortunately, however, progressive cities have found a better way. They have begun to apply to the management of the schools the scientific principles of engineering that have proved to be so successful in the management of big business enterprises.

Railroad companies locate their switches and terminals, and secure the necessary land, years ahead of the time when its need will become imperatively pressing. Industrial corporations secure their land for expansion and plan additions to their manufacturing and selling plants years before the time when their business will become handicapped in competition by cramped quarters. Telephone companies and banks select the sites and plan their branches to keep pace with the growth of the cities where they are operating, and the branches are ready when the business comes. Business men and public-spirited citizens in many progressive cities are now coming to realize that the schools constitute a basic factor in all economic de-.velopment and civic progress; and so in many of our cities, surveys of the. conditions and future needs for the school plant are being carried out; and provisions for properly located school sites, and for buildings adequately planned for modern school activities are being intelligently made.

With this new type of school policy in view; with a keen sense of the present congested condition of the school plant, and with the feeling that the problem of expansion must be solved and solved right, the Niles Board of Education, and its general manager, the Superintendent of Schools, have employed the writer to make a careful survey of the school housing conditions in Niles. The purpose of the survey is to assist them in outlining a building program that shall provide for the needs of a school system to be kept abreast of the times in quality, while expanding in size to meet adequately the needs of the growing city.

III. THE BUILDING PROBLEM DEFINED.

The first step in the survey was to get at the facts as to present conditions of congestion, as to the rate of growth of the school population and as to the directions in which the flow of population is tending. Accordingly, at the request of the Surveyor and with the assistance of the teachers and the secretary of the Board of Education, Superintendent Eby secured such data as to the school enrollments of 1915 and 1920 as were available, and had them tabulated by schools and grades according to the directions accompanying the request. He was asked also to have prepared at each school building a map of the city mounted on soft wood, on which the home of each child in attendance should be located. This was done by having each child, under the supervision of the teacher, stick a pin in the map at the point representing the location of his home.

By means of the tabulated enrollments and the pin-maps for the several schools and by means of careful inspections of all the buildings, it has been possible to determine the present conditions. Also by motoring over every part of the school district and beyond its boundaries in every direction it has been possible in connection with the pin maps, and with other information that was available, to get a good line on the geography of the city and the probable areas over which the population will flow during the next ten years. The data at hand enables us clearly to define the problem that the Board of Education is facing. There are two distinct phases of this problem.—

1. What must be done to meet the emergency presented by the increase of school enrolment that will certainly take place next fall?

2. What are the essential details of a building program that shall provide for the children, as fast as they come on, the necessary school sites and school buildings, each adequate in size, correctly located and affording all the facilities of a thoroughly modernized school?

In solving the first or emergency phase of the problem it is necessary to deal mainly with some temporary expedients such as are not to be thought of in connection with a permanent educational policy; while in solving the second, plans must be laid for a scientific expansion of the school plant during the coming decade. The present emergency must first be met; and then the plans for the coming ten-year period must be so made that when they are carried out, the board of education of fifteen and of twenty-five years hence shall inherit from the present no legacies of overcrowding, no inadequate or badly located sites, and no misfit or ill-planned buildings, such as the present board has to deal with. The Time to Do This Is Now; and So Favorable a Time Will Never Come Again.

CHAPTER II.

THE EMERGENCY AND HOW TO DEAL WITH IT

I. CONGESTION IN THE FIRST SIX GRADES.

Table 1 shows for each building what grades, if any, are now overcrowded. On scanning this table the following facts become apparent.

1. In Jefferson School there are only 6 pupils in excess of the number of seats, in two of the rooms; so that the congestion here does not look serious (column 9). However (column 10) there are in five rooms 31 seats in excess of the legal limits for these rooms, and (column 7) there are in six rooms 34 pupils in excess of the numbers for whom these rooms provide the amount of air space required by state law. (Compare columns 4 and 5. The law requires that 200 cubic feet per pupil be provided for grades I to IV, 225 for grades V to VIII, and 250 for grades IX to XII.) It might be thought that when congestion occurs in one room, pupils can be shifted to another where there is vacant space; but this is rarely possible, because those rooms are usually occupied by pupils of a different grade, who are older or younger and are doing entirely different work.

The congestion in Jefferson school is located in grades I and II, where there are 25 pupils in excess, and in grades V and VI, where there are 7 pupils in excess.

2 In Jackson school there are 17 more seats than the law allows; but at present only 5 pupils in excess of the legal limit. These are in the two 6th grade rooms.

3. In Lincoln school there are apparently only 4 pupils in excess of the legal limit; but by reference to column 11 it will be seen that there are 42 pupils of grade I to whom no seats are assigned. This grade of 102 children has been assigned to rooms 1 and 2—85 to Room 1 and 17 to Room 2, which they occupy along with 29 pupils of the 2d grade. The 85 pupils assigned to Room 1 are divided into two platoons on half-day sessions, 43 pupils attending three hours in the morning and the other 42 attending three hours in the afternoon. This form of platoon system is both inefficient and unpopular. Parents and pupils do not like it and school men tolerate it only in an emergency when there is no other remedy for congestion. Overcrowding in this building is prevented by restricting 85 pupils out of 398 to half-day sessions. The platoon system must not be confused with the Work—Study—Play plan.

4. In Garfield school there are 59 more pupils enrolled in that building than its four rooms provide for. These are now being taught in the upper hall and in a rented room, neither of which is fit for permanent occupancy. The Board of Education has accepted plans for a six-room addition to this building. This addition, if completed by the opening of school next fall, will take care of the excess pupils in this section of the city and also some from neighboring sections. Every possible effort should be made to have the additional class rooms ready on time.

5. The Monroe school is not congested, but is practically filled up. There is space for only 38 more pupils in its four rooms. See Column 7. The location of this school is very unfortunate on account of the noise and smoke from tracks of the Erie Railroad, which are separated from it only by the width of two vacant lots. In the rooms on the side toward the railroad, recitations cannot be carried on successfully while trains are passing, so there is much interruption of work throughout the day.

6. The Washington, or Old Central building, contains 8 available rooms, 5 of which are used for the shop and drawing work of the high school and the 3 remaining for a 4th, a 7th and an 8th grade. This building is not congested; but for other reasons that will be mentioned later, is not fit for housing school children; and its continued use for such a purpose can be defended only on the grounds of extreme necessity, as an emergency measure only.

7. The Grant building is a two-room structure on a small lot, the rooms being on the plan of the obsolete one-room rural school. It also is entirely unfit for the ordinary purposes of a modern city school. It houses in these two rooms a 1st and 2nd grade and is not over-crowded; but the 2nd grade is on half-day sessions on the platoon plan in order to share the room with a 3rd grade which also occupies it during half of each school day. This 3rd grade has 46 pupils. Overcrowding is preventing by restricting 89 pupils out of 131 to half-day sessions.

8. The Harrison building at McKinley Heights is a four-room structure, all of whose rooms are too small. It has 7 more pupils and 27 more seats than the air space required by law permits.

II. THE SOLUTION.

The accompanying table summarizes the number of pupils in excess of legal air space for all rooms in each of these buildings; and shows at a glance the buildings in which the congestion is, and in what grades the overflow is to be found.

Excess of Pupils in Grades I-VI Over Numbers for Whom Legally Acceptable Accommodations are Available—Distributed by Grades and Schools.

Schools	1	2	3	4	5	6	Total
Jefferson	10	15	--	2	3	4	34
Lincoln	42	--	--	2	1	1	46
Jackson	--	--	--	--	--	5	5
Garfield	--	37	22	--	--	--	59*
Grant	--	--	46	--	--	--	46
Harrison	--	3	3	1.	--	--	7
Totals 6 schools	52	55	71	5	4	10	197

Washington ------------	--	--	--	38	--	--	38
Grant -----------------	42	43	--	--	--	--	85
Totals** 8 schools ----	94	98	71	43	4	1⁰	320

* In upper hall and a rented room, both of which should be abandoned.

** Including pupils in Washington and Grant buildings, both of which should be abandoned.

It is worst in the three lowest grades and is about equally bad in four buildings, Jefferson, Lincoln, Garfield and Grant. There are in these six grades 197 more pupils than the available rooms now in use (that is including one at Washington and excluding the seated hall and rented room at Garfield) can normally provide for. This condition is bad; but some relief is at hand. The Roosevelt building with 8 rooms, capable of properly housing 306 pupils, will in all probability be in readiness next September. By means of careful adjustment of district boundaries, with the pin maps and the accompanying tabulations before him, the Superintendent can take care of the overflow from the crowded elementary buildings. There probably will be space for these and for the normal yearly increase in the enrolment of the first six grades; but a very real difficulty in re-adjusting will occur in avoiding the evil of sending children too far from their homes. It is necessary to say, however, that the Roosevelt building must be completed with all equipment in, and seats ready for occupancy at the opening of school next September. No more seats should be placed in this building than the numbers listed in column 7 of Table 1— namely 306.

More specifically, the status with reference to this phase of the problem is as follows:

Enrolment, all schools, grades I-VI, 1920 ---------------------1825

Enrolment, all schools, grades I-VI, 1915 ---------------------1162

Increase past 5 years 1915-1920 ------------------------------ 663

Percentage increase over 1915 ------------------------------- 57

Estimated increase 1920-1925 (57% of 1825) -------------------1040

Increase 1 year 1920-21 (1-5 of 1040) -------------------- 208

Excess of pupils at present ---------------------------------- 197

Excess pupils Sept. 1921 over present available capacity -------- 405

Less seats to be provided by Roosevelt building --------------- 306

Net excess Sept. 1921 --------------------------------------- 99

There is now an aggregate vacant legal seating capacity for 186 pupils (see Table I-A, Column 5), so scattered about the city in various buildings and rooms that most of it cannot now be used. This is because small odd lots of pupils from one grade cannot ordinarily be tau'ht in a room occupied by a higher or a lower grade. It seems fairly probable, however, that the net estimated excess of 99 pupils may be absorbed among these 186 vacant seats. It is not safe to count on such a contingency, however, and therefore no effort should be spared to get the Garfield addition finished, equipped and ready for occupancy along with the Roosevelt building by September next.

With Garfield addition completed, the status would be as given below:

New capacity Roosevelt building ------------------------------------ 306
New capacity Garfield building ------------------------------------- 228

Total new capacity Sept. 1921 -------------------------------------- 534
Less estimated excess of pupils over present available capacity -- 405

Net excess capacity Sept. 1921 ------------------------------------- 129
Less 1 room in Washington (46), and 2 in Grant (88) -------------- 134
Number of pupils in excess of capacity Sept. 1921 with both
    Roosevelt and Garfield addition in commission and with
    Washington and Grant abandoned ------------------------------ 5

Our assumption with reference to the rate of increase of pupils is the only factor involving doubt. If this rate holds for the present year as it has on the average for the past five years, there will be 5 more pupils than the number for which there will be available capacity. However, as in the estimate just preceding this one there is now in various scattered rooms capacity for 186 pupils which is not utilized; and it is probable that by careful study and shifting a considerable part of this unused capacity may be made available so as to absorb the small excess of pupils.

III. CONGESTION IN GRADES SEVEN TO TWELVE.

1. The Facts in the Case.

The most serious emergency problem with regard to overcrowding is in the 7th, 8th and 9th grades (Junior High School) and the 10th, 11th and 12th grades (Senior High School).

Six hundred ninety-eight pupils of these grades are now enrolled in the McKinley High School Building, which originally was designed and expected to accommodate not more than 507. See Table V, Column 6. I have made a careful survey of the building with reference to its pupil capacity. My analysis and calculations show that if we assume an average of 25 pupils per class (which is the standard) and also assume that every room and laboratory is in use by such a class for 85% of the running time, the building as it now stands can accommodate 663 (see Table 6) pupils. This represents its actual maximum capacity; for 85% efficiency in the planning and operation of the time schedule is about the best that can be attained if we assume that the schedule is based on a modern varied curriculum with departmental instruction and with full use of study halls, gymnasiums and laboratories during a six or seven-period day without resorting to the platoon system or to the Gary (work-study-play) system. By comparing the capacity as calculated (663) with the latest official enrolment (705) it will be observed that the building now actually holds forty-two more pupils than it is theoretically possible to crowd into it and at the same time operate it with reasonable educational efficiency on the usual plan of operation.

As a matter of fact and in confirmation of my calculations, it may be stated that in seven of the eight rooms occupied by grades 7 and 8, there are 48 more seats in use than the architect's blueprint prescribes; and there are in various rooms a total of 48 pupils in excess of the number for which air space is provided as required by state law. See Table I.

This, however, is not by any means the whole story. There are

/9 pupils of the 7th and 8th grades who ought to be housed with the others, but are now housed in the Washington or Old Central building; and there are also 3 shop rooms and a drawing room in this latter building that are being used by senior and junior high school pupils, who lose much time in going and coming between the two buildings, and ought to be accommodated at the McKinley building. It is quite clear therefore that at their present capacity, both the McKinley High School and the Old Central Building are now fully utilized and in fact overcrowded. Hence even assuming that the Old Central building, unsafe, insanitary and unhygienic as it is, were to be used next fall, there is no room available in either building to take care of the increase of approximately 177 pupils who will swell the enrolment in the six upper grades next September.

In taking account of the gains in school population due to increase in the population of the city and of the losses due to dropping out of school, I have used for grades VII and VIII the average percentage of gains in enrolment per pear for the past five years and the average of the percentage losses for the years 1915 and 1920. By applying these percentages to 276 for next year's 7th grade and 203 for next year's 8th grade, I estimate a net loss of 38 pupils for the former and a net loss of 19 pupils for the latter. This makes the probable 7th grade enrolment for next September 238 and the probable 8th grade enrolment 184. Adding these to 532, the estimated probable enrolment of grades IX-XII, we have for the probable enrolment in grades VII-XII next fall a total of 954 pupils which is an increase of 177 over the 777 now enrolled in the junior and senior high school grades. Supt. Eby's estimate based on reports from the teachers as to probable entrants next year gives 943—an increase of 166. I regard this estimate as conservative. For many reasons I think the actual increase will more likely exceed it than fall short of it. See Table 7.

We now have the emergency problem for next fall clearly before us. How can 177 additional pupils be taken care of next fall in grades VII to XII when McKinley High School building and the Old Central Building are already being utilizeed to the full extent of their possible pupil capacity, and with seven rooms seating 48 more pupils than the law allows?

2. Plans to Meet the Emergency.

To accommodate 177 additional pupils on the present plan of operation will require seven rooms (classrooms or shops or laboratories) in addition to those now in use in both buildings. It is clear therefore that the administration must either provide seven new rooms by September next, or change the plan of operation and provide some new rooms.

There seems to be four and only four plans that are at all feasible, as follows:

Plan I. Provide seven modern unit movable school rooms and place them on the McKinley lot.

Plan II. Remodel the outdoor gymnasium at the rear of the McKinley building, making a machine shop, a wood shop and a cafeteria on the first floor, and a wood shop, a drawing and art room, and a print shop on the second floor. Each of these rooms might have floor area of 40 or 45x24 feet, and this would leave adequate space for hall and stairways and two small storage rooms over the hall. Remove the shops at the Old Central building to this new shop building and reseat the old shop rooms. This will provide 8 class rooms instead of 3 in the Old Central building. House the entire 7th grade in these rooms and grades VIII-XII at McKinley High school building.

Plan III. Organize the entire school, grades VII-XII into two or three platoons. Make a 9-period time table with two lunch periods in the middle of the day. Arrange the time schedule so that not more than two-thirds of the classes shall be in school at any one time. Build the new shops and cafeteria and use them. Abandon entirely the Washington or Old Central building.

Plan IV. Build the new shops and cafeteria as in Plans II and III and abandon entirely the Washington building. Organize and operate the school on the "Work-Study-Play" plan, arranging the schedule so that half the school shall be in the class rooms while the other half is distributed about equally among (1) the shops and laboratories; (2) the gymnasium, study rooms and playground, and (3) the auditorium. With this plan it will be necessary to provide two additional class rooms in order to provide for the balanced organization. This can be done by dividing the large room number 9 and also the proposed drawing and art room each into two rooms by means of temporary partitions.

3. Discussion of the Emergency Plans.

Plan I has many disadvantages. In the first place movable buildings represent only a temporary expedient to meet congestion, but their use tends to become a habit; and it is a very bad habit when it becomes fixed. When resorted to it seems an easy way of putting off the only permanent solution, namely a building plan and policy, which like that of our national navy, must look years ahead and provide for a continuous state of preparedness and efficiency. This is the only way to prevent disasters and make wasteful expedients unnecessary. Resorting to portables is like easing pain with aspirin, which makes one unconscious of disease until the system is broken down and ruined beyond hope.

In the second place portables are unpopular with the parents of the children who have to occupy them, and rightly so; because they are unhomelike, are not capable of the best heating and ventilation, and are apt to be so crowded on the school lot that they interfere seriously with one another in securing adequate daylight. Also they fill up the school grounds and leave little or no playground space for the pupils—thus depriving the latter of a part of the birthright of every child. In the third place portables are unprofitable as an investment, both because of the previously stated objections and because they are relatively expensive. Six of these movables would cost from six to nine thousand dollars—a sum which would go a long way toward building over the outdoor gymnasium into a very good shop building.

My judgment is strongly against the portables excepting in certain rare cases where only one or two are needed for a short time; and I therefore advise that Plan I be ruled out.

Plan II will effectively take care of the emergency for next fall; but is open to serious objections. First, it involves segregating the

7th grade from the remainder of the Junior High School. This will cause serious loss of esprit-de-corps, will increase the difficulties of supervision, and will seriously interfere with the features of departmental instruction and promotion by subjects, which are essential to the best working of a junior high school organization.

It also involves the continued use of the Washington building which is unfit for use as a school building and should be permanently abandoned as a day school at the earliest possible date. I therefore advise that Plan II be ruled out. This leaves the choice only between Plan III and Plan IV.

Plan III is entirely feasible; and will work fairly well; but the platoon system is not capable of subserving the best interest of the children. It shortens their time in school and leaves them too much of their time away from the supervision and direction of their teachers. Most of their studying must be done out of school. Now it is well known in the experience of school men that children when out of school are likely to be on the streets more than at home. The parents of most children do not see to it that they have regular hours of home duties, study and harmless and profitable play; so when the children are out of school during a larger portion of the day than is usual, they waste much of their time and contract idle or mischievous habits.

Furthermore the school becomes very loosely organized when attending in platoons; and it is difficult to maintain unity of school spirit and solidarity of purpose among both students and teachers.

Finally the platoon system tends to disorganize the family life especially when children in the same family attend during different hours.

Plan IV Is Recommended for Adoption.

For these reasons and since the choice is now narrowed down to that between Plan III and Plan IV, I am inclined to advise against Plan III and in favor of Plan IV, which has none of the objections of the first three plans, is not a temporary expedient, but a well tried plan which is being adopted as a permanent policy in many progressive school systems, and has many and real advantages of peculiar merit.

The "Work-Study-Play" system which only the installation of the new shop rooms will make possible, is therefore recommended for adoption.

CHAPTER III.

THE PROBLEM OF THE BUILDING PROGRAM

I.   FORECASTING THE INCREASES IN ENROLMENT.

In order to know definitely how many buildings Niles will need immediately and in the near future, to house both the present excess of children and the increasing numbers who are coming on, we should be able to predict how many more children there will be, say, in September 1925 than there are now. To do this with accuracy would be very difficult, if not impossible. It is possible, however, to make an approximate estimate based on the data that are available. This I shall try to do; for an estimate made on the basis of any reliable data, even though meagre, is far better than a mere guess out of the blue sky, however shrewd the guess might be. In Table II, we have the enrolments for all grades for the years 1915 and 1920, as follows:

	Enrolments 1915	1920	5 year increase	% increase 5 years.
Grades I-VIII _____	1432	2210	778	54.3
Grades IX-XII _____	316	400	84	27.0

The distribution of these enrolments is given both by buildings and by grades in Table II and are summarized in Table II-A.

If we assume that these rates of increase in the various grades for the past five-year period will continue in the average for the coming five-year period, we can estimate the increase up to September 1925, by taking 54% of 2,210, the 1920 enrolment for grades I-VIII, and adding to it 27% of the 1920 enrolment of grades IX-XII. The result is 1,193 plus 108, or 1,301 for the entire city and all grades.

Of course it is by no means certain that the school population will continue to grow for the next five or ten years at exactly the same rate at which it has increased for the past five years. The rate may gradually diminish; but on the other hand it may increase. This rate of growth has on the average added to the enrolment 260 pupils per year. The increase of pupils for next year over the present enrolment will almost certainly exceed 300; so there is no indication in the experience of the past or present that should lead us to discount this figure in forecasting the future.

As a further check on this estimate, however, we may compare the rate of increase of the school enrolment with the rates of increase in the total city population and the enumeration of youth of school age. The population increased during the past ten year period 56%, an average rate of increase of 5.6% per year. The enumerated youth increased during the past nine years 32.6%, an average rate of 3.6% per year. Under perfectly normal and stable conditions, the school enrolment should have approximately the same rate of increase as the total population and as that of the enumerated youth. That is, the three numbers should bear a constant ratio to one another. It is quite clear however, that for one cause or another they have not done this. The rate of increase for the combined elementary and high school enrolment is 9.8% per year or nearly twice that for the population and more than twice that for the enumeration.

There may therefore be considerable ground for supposing that our estimated average increase in enrolment of 260 pupils per year is too high; but in my opinion it is unsafe to base the building program on a lower estimate. We cannotbe sure that the present rate will become smaller; and there are as many reasons for conjecturing that it may become larger as there are for thinking that it may diminish.

Hence it is safer to accept 260 pupils per year for the average rate at which the enrolment will increase than it would be to base the building program on either a smaller or a larger rate. In my opinion this rate is sufficiently conservative; and the adoption of a smaller one might lead to unwise expenditure by investing large sums in buildings likely to prove themselves inefficient by reason of being too small, on the other hand, the erection of too large a building would involve waste also, altho this waste would last only while the population was growing up to the building. The erection of buildings in small units would interfere with a progressive development of the educational program in a manner much more serious than any but an an expert in school administration is likely to foresee. The administration is even now finding itself handicapped in operating the schools on modern principles because the small buildings necessitate handling the children in small groups. It is difficult, for an example, to introduce the feature of semi-annual promotions, and the feature of grouping pupils according to ability instead of according to age or to years in school.

The use of small buildings also involves ultimately a large waste of funds by failure to take advantage of the greater economy that results from the use of large buildings. **Hence, from the standpoints of both efficiency, in the educational program, and of ultimate economy of expenditure in the building program the policy of building in larger units should prevail.**

One reason why we may very well expect a larger rate of increase in enrolment than a smaller is worthy of specific mention here. The losses by reason of pupils leaving school before completing the curriculum are decreasing. In the High School especially, the success of the administrative and teaching staff in holding the pupils longer in school has been remarkable. This success has been due to definite, united, and effective effort with this end in view, an effort and a policy for which great credit should be given to the superintendent, the high school principal, and the teaching staff. The effect of this policy will be increased by 'he use of larger, more commodious and more attractive modern building units including auditoriums, libraries, laboratories and adequate play-grounds and gymnasiums. The important modern facilities can be incorporated in large buildings with relatively small additional expense; but their cost when duplicated in many small buildings is likely to become prohibitive, so that most of the pupils in the city will be deprived of them. Furthermore, experience in many other communities has proved that when new and attractive buildings are installed, with modern courses of study including vocational and pre-vocational studies, such buildings always fill up and become crowded much more promptly than was expected. The reasons for this are two: First, pupils of the community are attracted into the schools, who otherwise would not come, and second, people with families of children to be educated are attracted to the city by its superior educational advantages, and move in from other communities. **Such people constitute a valuable asset to any city because of their superior intelligence, ambition, and industry.**

With these considerations in view, I have worked out the building program which I shall recommend on the basis of expectation of an average yearly increase of 260 in the enrolment; and have so planned as to make liberal allowance for a possible increase in this rate, as well as for a possible shrinkage.

II. CALCULATING THE ADDITIONAL PUPIL CAPACITY REQUIRED.

The analysis and calculation based on the data set forth in Tables I, II and II-A, show that there is a net excess pupils over the pupil capacity of the present buildings of 339 pupils, (See Table III, Column 6, 7.) This is the result arrived at on the assumption that all rooms not fit for use according to state building standards are to be abandoned as soon as this is feasible. The pupil capacity thus eliminated would amount to 339 pupils. (See Table III, Column 3.)

The increase in enrolment, calculated on the basis of the data set forth in Tables I and II, will, by September of the year 1925, amount to 1,301 pupils. The only element of doubt in this estimate is that which arises from assuming 54% and 27% as the average rates of increase in enrolments for the elementary and high school grades respectively. The grounds for adopting these rates have been fully examined above. If these rates be accepted; and if it be admitted that the unfit rooms are to be abandoned, our building arrangements must provide capacity for 339 plus 1302=1640 pupils.

The Roosevelt building, now nearing completion, and the Garfield addition, for which plans have been accepted, will provide standard accommodations for 306 and 228 pupils respectively, or an aggregate of 534. Subtracting this number from 1640, the excess just stated, we have a net prospective excess of pupils over capacity of 1106 pupils, which is the number that the building program to be recommended must provide for. At an average of 40 pupils to the room, this would take 28 new rooms. At an average of 35 pupils per room, which would be a better basis from the educational standpoint, because junior and senior high school classes must be smaller than classes in grades I-VI, the number of new rooms to be provided would be 32. (For detailed analysis see Table III.)

The next step in the building problem is to find out where the new rooms should be located.

III. DETERMINING WHERE TO PLACE NEW BUILDING UNITS.

In solving this part of the problem, the pin-maps mentioned early in this report supplied the only available data; but fortunately the inferences to be drawn from these maps are quite clear.

A count was made on the map for each school, of the pins in each of the various sections of the city. The result of this count is shown in Table IV, in which each horizontal line represents a school named at the left, and each vertical column represents one of the distinct geographical sections of the city, as follows:

1-A. The section to the west of Mosquito Creek and north of the Erie and B. & O. R. R. tracks.

1-B. The section to the west of Mosquito Creek and south of the Erie and B. & O. R. R. tracks.   ·

2-A. The section to the east of Mosquito Creek and to the west of Vienna Avenue.

2-B. The section to the east of Vienna Avenue and north of Robbins Avenue.

3. The section to the north and east of the Erie and B. & O. R. R. tracks and south of Robbins Avenue.

4. "Loop." The section to the east of Mosquito Creek, lying to the south of the Erie and B. & O. R. R. tracks and to the north of the Mahoning River.

5. The section to the south of the Mahoning river.

From the figures in Table IV. it may be seen how many pupils now attending any one school live in each of these sections of the city.

The following tabulation summarizes these figures, and shows the number of pupils from the eastern sections (including one-half the "loop" section—who are enrolled in senior high school (Column 2), in junior high school (Column 3), and in all the schools (Column 4).

GEOGRAPHICAL DISTRIBUTION OF PUPILS IN THE
CITY OF NILES 1920-1921

1	2	3	4
School	Senior	Junior	All
	High	High	Schools
Section of the city	School	School	United
2-A _____	40	49	185
2-B _____	110	92	541
3 _____	20	49	439
Harrison _____	---	8	140
Loop (½) _____	2	24	162
Grant _____	---	---	170
Totals—Eastern sections _____	172	222	1547
Total in each school group _____	327	393	2549
Percent those living in eastern sections are			
of entire school groups _____	52.6	56 5	60.7

Thus of the 327 senior high school pupils who registered on the pin-map, 172 or 52.6% live east of Mosquito Creek, excluding the eastern half of the "loop" section. Similarly it is revealed that 56.5% of the junior high school pupils and 60.7% of all the pupils in all the schools live east of Mosquito Creek exclusive of the western half of the loop section. The western half of this latter section, the whole of which is cut off from the remainder of the city by the railroad tracks, has been grouped with the sections to the west of Mosquito Creek because this portion of the loop section is more accessible to the western division of the city than to the eastern division.

The pin map registration checks very closely with the enrolment figures for all the schools excepting the senior high school, where complete registration was not secured. There will result from this no error of serious proportions, however, if we assumed that the 52.6% of those who did register on the map and who live in the eastern sections are typical of the entire enrolment. That is, we may safely assume that if the pin map registration of the senior high school were complete, we should still find that 53% or more reside east of Mosquito Creek.

From the character of the homes recently erected and now building, and from the character of the allotments being placed on the homesite market, it seems quite evident that the prevailing tendency of the well-to-do and middle-class citizens, the sort of people who are accustomed to sending their children to the high school—are gravitating toward this eastern section in greater proportion than toward the other sections. It seems probable therefore, that within five years the percentage of the high school enrolment from this section will rise and overtake that of all the grades taken collectively. That is, we may fairly expect that from 60 to 70 per cent of the excess enrolment of all grades by 1925-6, or about two-thirds, will reside in the eastern section of the city. Getting down to figures, our estimated excess in enrolment over present accommodations was 1,640 pupils; and approximately two-thirds of these, or 1,093 will reside in the eastern sections and the remaining one-third or 547, will reside in the western sections.

It will be recalled that Roosevelt and the Garfield addition will take care of 534 pupils, while for the remainder of the excess, namely 1,106 pupils, no buildings are as yet either erected or planned.

In other words, the estimated excess for the year 1925 on the west side is 546 pupils, and of these by a fortunate coincidence, 534 will be provided with accommodations in rooms already built or planned. On the other hand, 1,093 pupils, according to our estimate, will reside on the east side; and for these as yet no rooms are even projected. **Our building program therefore must provide for approximately 1,100 pupils by 1925, and the rooms for their accommodation must be located to the east of Mosquito Creek.**

IV. DETERMINING CAPACITY. LOCATION, AND CHARACTER OF
THE BUILDING UNITS IMMEDIATELY REQUIRED.

Our estimated east side enrolment for 1925 shows us that by that time we should have school housing accommodations on the east side for 1,100 pupils; and the foregoing discussion brings us to the conclusion that one large building unit will be much more economical in the end and also vastly more efficient educationally than two or three smaller units would be.

Let us now make an estimate as to how fast one large building will fill up.

The present excess over legal standard capacity is 339 pupils, according to the indications of the pin-map study; two-thirds of these, or 226, should attend school on the east side. Also the average increase of the total enrolment was estimated at 260 pupils per year and two-thirds of these, 174, should attend school on the east side. We have then the following table for the probable east side enrolments up to 1925.

Date	Excess		Increase		Total capacity required
September 1921 _____	226	+	174	=	400
September 1922 _____	400	+	174	=	574
September 1923 _____	574	+	174	=	748
September 1924 _____	748	+	174	=	922
September 1925 _____	922	+	174	=	1096

According to this estimate. it is clear that if a small building were erected it would be filled up by September 1922; and another small building would be in immediate demand to prevent over-crowding. On the other hand, if a building to accommodate a thousand to twelve hundred pupils be erected it will be filled to half its capacity in 1922 and to three-fourths of its capacity in 1923. By 1925 it will be filled to capacity and another building must then be under way. As this building cannot be ready before September 1922, the loss in interest on the capital invested by reason of the space temporarily not used will not be serious, and will be practically non-existent in two years after the completion of the building. There seem therefore to be scarcely any arguments in favor of small buildings and very many in favor of the immedi-ate projection of a large building. If the large building be accepted as the choice of the city and the Board of Education, it is evident. also that it must provide for the junior high school grades, namely VII, VIII and IX, as well as for the first six grades. In other words, the building must be of such a character that it may provide for a complete nine-grade school, rather than for either an ex-clusive junior high school or an exclusive six-grade elementary school.

I therefore recommend, that the first step in the building program be the erection of a nine-grade schoolhouse with all modern feat-ures; and I further recommend that this building be so planned that later on it ay include a senior high school with grades X, XI and XII. When this is done, of course, the capacity required for the senior high school must be formed by excluding a sufficient number of elementary grade pupils and providing space for the latter in other buildings. The plans, therefore, should be made with this prospective change in view.

This building should be located not less than two miles nor more than two and a half miles from McKinley High School. It should be near enough to Robbins Avenue to be convenient to the car line, especially in bad weather, and far enough removed from it to avoid the noise and dust of the street traffic. .

V. UNITS THAT WILL BE NEEDED LATER.

1. The East Side.

The building already recommended which, for the sake of brevity, we may call number 11, will meet the requirements of the east side for the elementary and junior high school grades until 1925, the senior high school pupils, grades X-XII, from this section should continue at McKinley, where there will be room for them on account of the withdrawal from this building of all junior high school pupils from the east side. When McKinley again becomes crowded the east side senior high school pupils may be transferred to number 11.

Probably some time between 1925 and 1927 number 11 will be filled, and an elementary building for the first six or the first nine grades will be required to be placed in section 2-B to the north and east of Lincoln school and to the north and west of number 11. The next step in the development on the east side will be necessitated by the growth eastward of section 3. This step will be an addition to the Jefferson building where there is sufficient land and where the plan of the present building admits of an addition that can be so planned as to convert this into a modern school plant with accommodations for twice or possibly nearly three times the number of pupils that is now housed there.

This building which I shall call the Jefferson addition, should not be needed before 1935 unless it turns out that in section 3 the school population grows much faster than in section 2-B. In that case the Jefferson addition and our number 13 would have to change places in the building program. This completes the building program for the east side as far as it is either possible or necessary to outline it. Let us now direct our attention to the west side.

2. The West Side.

Roosevelt building will provide for all the children who reside in Section 1-A for ten or fifteen years to come, provided that pupils from other sections are removed from it to keep pace with the growth of enrolment from pupils living in that section. Its capacity can be doubled by an addition when this becomes necessary.

Garfield building with its projected addition will take care of the growth in enrolment in Grades I-VI of Section 4, at the present rate of increase for those grades until 1931, provided as in the case of Roosevelt, the pupils from other sections are removed from this building according as the school population in Section 4 increases.

This leaves of the west side only Section 1-B to consider. The present enrolment of pupils in Grades I-VI residing in this section is 258, while the only elementary building in the section is Jackson, with a legal standard capacity of 369.

Assuming that for the immediate future the excess of pupils in the loop section over the capacity of Monroe building will be divided about equally between the east side and the west side sections and that the elementary grade now in the Washington building must also be included in Section 1-B. We have the following statement for the balance of pupils against accommodations in this section.

Building	Section City	Standard Capacity	Pin-map Registration Grades I-VI	Pupils who can be accommodated
Jackson	1 B	369	---	---
Scattered	1 B	---	258	---
Washington	1 B	---	37	---
Monroe	"Loop"	180	---	---
Scattered	"Loop" (½)	---	136	ˉ431
Excess	1 B & ½Loop	---	---	118
Total	1 B & ½Loop	549	---	549

It thus appears that there are accommodations to Grades I-VI for 118 more pupils in Monroe and Jackson, belonging than there are pupils so located in the city that they should attend school in Section 1-B. The forecast for increased enrolment in this section, like that for the others, is based on the percentage increase of the first six grades during the past five years. This we found, in Table II-A to be 57%. The combined enrolments include 431 pupils. The probable increase for the next five-year period is 57% of 431=247, an average of 1-5 of 247 or 49 pupils per year.

On this basis the enrolments for the successive years should be approximately as follows:

1921	431+49=480	1926	676+49=725
1922	480+49=529	1927	725+49=774
1923	529+49=578	1928	774+49=823
1924	578+49=627	1929	823+49=872
1925	627+49=676	1930	872+49=921

From this it seems that the enrolment will not exceed the capacity in this section before 1923; and it is probable that by placing in the Roosevelt and Garfield buildings pupils from this section who live near those buildings, overcrowding in Jackson building can be avoided until about 1924 or 1925. It will then be necessary,—especially if that section continues to grow as would seem likely—to plan for a new building for a nine-grade school in Section 1-B.

By 1930 we should expect the enrolment of this section in Grades I-VI to reach 921. On the basis of the rate at which they are now growing, the junior high school grades VII-IX, should have increased about 350, 1-3 of which increase or 116 would belong in this section. Adding 116 to 921 we have a total of 1,037 pupils or 488 more than the capacity of Jackson and Monroe.

If these figures indicate approximately the actual conditions of ten years hence, it will be seen that the new west side building bould be ready about 1925 and if planned for 500 pupils it would be filled up by 1931. Hence, if by 1924 the growth of the school enrolments goes along substantially as is indicated above, it clearly would be good policy at that time to plan a building for 750 pupils, which would not fill up until 1935. The building might be so planned as to be erected in three successive sections.

This building should be located about a mile or a mile and a half west of the Jackson building and near, but not on Warren Avenue. For convenience of reference I shall call it number 12.

VI. SUMMARY OF THE BUILDING PROGRAM.

In view of the facts and inferences which have been set forth in detail, the various steps in the building program which is recommended are as follows:

Step 1. Proceed immediately to plan for the financing and erection on the east side of schoolhouse number 11, a modern plant for a nine-grade school, capable of being used ultimately for a twelve-grade school and having a maximum capacity of 1,200 pupils.

Step 2. About 1924, plan for the financing and erection of schoolhouse number 12, a nine-grade building having a maximum capacity of 750 pupils.

Step 3. About 1937, if the growth of the northern section of the east side indicates the need of additional accommodations plan for the financing and erection of a six or nine-grade, up-to-date schoolhouse,—number 13 in that section to the north and east of the Lincoln building.

Step 4. About 1934, if the demand has become evident, plan for the erection and financing of the Jefferson addition converting this building into an up-to-date plant for nine grades. It may turn out that steps 3 and 4 will have to change places.

With regard to the "Loop" section of the city, on account of its peculiar character and location, no predictions of any value can be made. For this district a watchful waiting policy should be adopted, which will be outlined and explained in a later section.

In the meantime all buildings and grounds should be put in perfect repair and maintained in the best possible condition.

CHAPTER IV.

BUILDINGS AND BUILDING SITES

I. THE PROPOSED EAST SIDE BUILDING, NO. 11.

With reference to this building, the policy recommended in Chapter III is to plan it for a modern fireproof nine-grade school. That is to say a school comprising a six-grade elementary organization and a junior high school organization including Grades VII, VIII and IX.

Furthermore if properly planned, and honestly constructed according to the best manner known to modern architectural engineering, this structure ought to last for a hundred years or more. In fact, if kept always in prime repair it is difficult to imagine any reason why it should not endure for several centuries, like the college buildings, cathedrals and palaces of the old world.

This being the case, we should not limit our vision of the future to five or ten years, but should consider the probable relations of this building to the school system at a time twenty, thirty or forty years hence.

It is the lack of such prophetic vision in the past that has placed so many of our cities in the sad predicament in which they now find themselves. One eastern city, for example, must immediately scrap every elementary building that it owns, and build new; because these buildings were erected according to a hand-to-mouth policy which failed utterly to take future needs into consideration.

With the ultimate needs of Niles in mind, therefor, it must be evident that if her growth continues as her business men think it will, and as all indications foreshadow, there is going to be need of an east side senior high school with other east side junior high schools tributary to it.

This building, Number 11, which is needed now for elementary and junior high school building in the location that I have designated, will be needed some time between fifteen and thirty years hence to house a senior high school. Nobody at this time can predict just WHEN it will be so needed; but no intelligent person who has faith in Niles and her future prospects of growth and prosperity can doubt for a moment that a part, if not all, of it WILL be needed for that very purpose. We must view this building as a permanent investment for Niles, and not as an item of current expense.

If this be granted, it is evident that tens of thousands of dollars can be saved for the children of Niles, who will be the tax payers fifteen or thirty years hence, by planning this building so that it can be used to house this prospective senior high school organization when it materializes. All that is necessary to accomplish this is to provide in the plans, rooms properly designed and located for such additional shops, laboratories and other special rooms as are characteristic of a modern comprehensive high school. These rooms can easily be planned so as to be added on, when needed, as rearward extensions of the two wings of the building.

1. The Architectural Problem.

The general problem of designing the building is now clearly before us. The following provisions are essential:'

    a. Space for a maximum of 1,200 children.

    b. Design and allotment of rooms of the proper size, character and location for the activities of an organization consisting of six elementary grades and three junior high school grades.

    c. The plans to be so made that 16-18 additional units (shops, laboratories and demonstration rooms, senior high school science and vocational work) may be built on at the rear of the two wings at a later time when they will be demanded. '

    d. The exterior of the building should be adapted to the needs of the interior and not vice versa. The design should not be extravagant and ornate, but both simple and artistic, becoming a manufacturing city with practical but artistic ideals.

    e. The grounds should be ample for play, athletics and school gardening; and that part of them immediately adjacent to the building should be landscaped and decorated with lawn, trees and shrubbery, according to the best artistic standards so that the school and school grounds may be a source of pride and satisfaction as well as a means of artistic education both to the children in attendance, and to the citizens of the community.

These requisites are not difficult of attainment; but will require the service of an architect who, by reason of long and varied experience in designing modern school plants, is familiar with the needs of modern balanced school organizations. They will also demand generous and enlightened, but not extravagant financing.

2. What the Plans Should Include.

The following outline shows the essential elements of the plan.

Essential Units of Plan for Building No. 11.

Number and Kinds of Rooms	Pupil Capacity	Capacity by Groups
16 Classrooms ----------------------------	625	625
2 Gymnasiums ----------------------------	80	
2 Study halls and library ----------------	240	320
3 Laboratories ----------------------------	75	
3 Shops ----------------------------------	75	
1 Mechanical drawing room --------------	25	
2 Commercial rooms ---------------------	50	
1 Art room -------------------------------	25-40	
1 Music room -----------------------------	25-40	275-320
1 Auditorium -----------------------------	800	800
1 Cafeteria and 1 lunch room -----------	400	400

Approximate Total Capacity as a Nine Grade School.

On the traditional plan of operation ------------------------- 750

On the work-study-play plan of operation -------------------- 1250

Additional Units to be Planned for Senior High School But Not to be Built.

Laboratories, Physics, Chemistry, Geography, Biology, Dressmaking, Millinery ---------------------------	6 units
Recitation Rooms supplementary to Laboratories ------	2 units
Shops ---	8-10 units

3. Description of the Types of Rooms.

1. The Classrooms. The 16 classrooms will provide two rooms for each of the first six elementary grades, three rooms for the three junior high school grades and one room for a kindergarten. Each classroom should have a capacity of approximately 8,000 cubic feet, and a floor surface of approximately 640 square feet. According to the requirements of the Ohio Statutes, this space would accommodate 40 pupils of the first four grades, 35 pupils of Grades V-VIII, or 32 pupils of Grades IX-XII.

If the administration policy should be to handle the children in larger classrooms, say of 45 instead of 40 in Grades I-IV, the classroom unit should be 9,000 cubic feet instead of 8,000. Such a policy would economize in teaching force; but with a corresponding reduction in educational efficiency.

2. The Gymnasiums. These should have a combined floor space 60 x 80 feet or 4,800 square feet, and should consist of a single room divided at the middle of the long axis by a rolling partition, so that one-half can be used exclusively for girls and the other exclusively for boys at the same time. For exhibition and contest purposes the two can be thrown together. There should be a continuous gallery with a padded running track, and raised seats for spectators. There should of course be separate showers, locker rooms and toilets for the boys and the girls adjoining the opposite ends, and also a swimming pool to be used at different times during the week by the boys and the girls respectively and on

different evenings during the week by the men and women of the community.

3. Study halls and library. These should occupy a central position in the building. Each room should comprise two units of capacity, or about 18,000 cubic feet. The library should occupy the middle position, and the two study halls should open into the library as well as into the corridor. Each room would accommodate 80 pupils. In the interest of flexibility of use and adaptation to unforeseen conditions, it would be very desirable so to design the two study halls that each can be divided in halves by means of a rolling partition in order that it may at any time be converted into two classrooms.

4. The Laboratories. These should include a nature study laboratory with a plant conservatory and garden plot adjoining outside, a cooking laboratory with the store room and laundry room adjoining, and a sewing laboratory with a fitting room adjoining. Each should be designed and equipped to accommodate a minimum of 25 pupils with some provision for expansion of equipment in case the need should arise.

5. The Shops. These should include a wood-working shop with stockroom and wood-working machine room adjoining, and arts and crafts shop with adjoining stock room, and a print shop with a small adjoining room which could be used as a designing or general utility room, and later perhaps converted into a room for photo-engraving and lithographing.

6. The Mechanical Drawing room. The mechanical drawing room should be near the wood shop, and the art room near the arts and crafts and print shops. Each of these rooms should be equipped for a minimum of 25 pupils.

7. The Commercial rooms. These should be adjoining with a commercial teacher's office between. The partitions between this office and the two rooms respectively should be of glass, so that the teacher may readily oversee the pupils in either room while he is in the office. One of these rooms should be equipped for book-keeping and office training and the other for typing.

8. The Art room. This should be artistically decorated, and equipped with drawing tables for 25 pupils. It should be large enough to permit the addition later of ten or fifteen more individual tables. There should be ample banks of lockers and drawing board racks, and cabinets for safe keeping of the pupils' drawing and color materials. There should be portfolio cabinets and display racks for keeping and displaying work done by the pupils, and a stock room for the safe keeping of drawing paper and extra materials.

9. The Music room should be equipped with a piano, a phonograph and a small stage and with lecture seats for 40 pupils. It should also be provided with a screen and a lantern. It could thus be used as a general lecture room and a room for dramatic rehearsals as well as a music room. The equipment should also include cabinets for musical instruments, player piano rolls and lantern slides. The windows should be provided with opaque blinds or curtains in addition to the usual adjustable shades.

10. The Auditorium. This room should seat about 800 persons, and have a full stage equipment and dressing rooms.

A moving picture booth and screen mounting should be included in the design.

11. The Cafeteria and lunch room. These should be adjacent, with a kitchen between of sufficient capacity to serve milk, cocoa and other lunch accessories to those children who carry their luncheons as well as to supply the regular kitchen service to the cafeteria.

The combined capacity of the cafeteria and lunch room should be sufficient for the accommodation of 800 pupils in two or three shifts.

12. General considerations. All rooms especially shops laboratories and other special rooms should be equipped with wash stands and running water.

All windows excepting those facing north (and of these there should be very few) should be equipped with semi-transparent adjustable shades of the Draper type.

The walls should be decorated with a "flat" oil paint. Rooms facing north should be colored a strong daffodil yellow. Rooms likely to have strong light are best decorated in a light soft tone of brown. For the walls of corridors and for some of the laboratories and shops a plaster finish is less desirable than light cream or yellow faced brick. Glazed brick that will not take pencil marks easily is best for the walls of toilet rooms.

Corridors and stairways should be so designed that they can receive adequate daylight on bright days and can be well lighted artificially on dark days.

The lighting of all rooms excepting possibly some shops and laboratories should be from the left only. The windows should be massed with narrow beveled mullions between and the most forward window should be at least five feet from the front wall. Tops of windows should reach to as near the ceiling as construction will permit—in any case not more than 8 inches from it. Lower sills of windows should be from three to four feet above floors. The total clear glass window area should equal not less than one-fifth of the floor area and the width of that part of the room which is used for writing and reading should not be greater than twice the height of the tops of the window sashes above the floor.

Since the height of the ceilings should not be much over 12½ feet this rule limits the width of a classroom to 24 feet or 25 feet. It would be well to make a few of the classrooms a little larger than the others; and place the windows of each in two groups rather than one; so that any of these large rooms could be divided by a partition into two small recitation rooms in case of future needs in connection with the prospective senior high school.

Every classroom should have a built-in storage closet a built-in case for specimens and books and a reading table near the bookcase. There should be a display board for pictures, clippings, etc., and a display moulding above the blackboard. The height and width of the blackboards should be adapted to the average height of the grade of pupils using the room. Blackboards should be of the best quality of black slate: any other quality is a very bad investment.

The following are the approved data for blackboards:

Grades	Width	Height of lower edge from floor
I and II _____	36 inches	24-26 inches
III and IV _____	36 "	26-28 "
V and VI _____	36 "	28-30 "
VII and VIII _____	42 "	30-34 "
IX to XII _____	42 "	34-36 "
Teacher's board _____	48 "	36 "

The floor plans should include ample space for the principal's office, a large outer office or lobby, a record vault and toilet room. A small separate office for the stenographer clerk separated from the lobby by a glass partition is also very desirable.

Space should be provided in the plans for 2 teachers' retiring rooms, 2 pupils' retiring rooms, a clinic room and one or two committee rooms and offices for pupils' organizations. These latter should be so located in the building as to be under easy observation by teachers or administrative assistants.

There should, of course, be adequate locker space and ample toilet facilities on each floor and bicycle rooms in the basement.

13. Cost. The cost of this building at present (1921) prices would be somewhere in the neighborhood of $450,000 to $500,000.

14. Later provisions for a Senior high school. The additional laboratories and shops that will be needed ultimately to provide for a complete and comprehensive senior high school organization are as follows:

Physical Science Group.—physics laboratory, chemistry laboratory with supplementary demonstration-recitation room and store rooms.　　3 units.

Biology—Geography Groups. Biology laboratory, geography laboratory, with supplementary demonstration-recitation room and store rooms.　　3 units.

Household Arts Group.—Dressmaking laboratory, millinery laboratory, with fitting and stock room.　　2 units.

Shop Group.—Machine shop, automobile shop, forge shop, sheet metal shop, with stock and tool rooms.　　6 units.

Woodworking shop, wood turning and pattern-making shop and house-framing shop with stock and tool rooms.　　4 units.

The plans should provide as completely as possible for the placing of all shops in one wing and all laboratory groups in the other wing, in order that the noise of the shops shall disturb the work of the classrooms as little as possible.

15. Adequacy of the plans. If the plans for this building are carefully worked out on the lines suggested with the additional senior high school units all provided for so that they may be built on when needed, the building will, in my opinion, be flexible enough to be adapted to every purpose for which it will be needed. It will afford facilities for every kind of school activity that the most enterprising and forward-looking manufacturing community

is likely to want, and at a much smaller ultimate outlay than if these were to be provided for by smaller special type buildings.

II. SITES.

1. Size and Cost.

The site for such a building as has been proposed should include an area certainly not less than 400 x 300 feet; and it should be as much larger as possible. Undoubtedly the land can be had now for less than it ever can be obtained later, and it would be a most regrettable mistake not to get enough while the getting is fairly good. It should be borne in mind that a city must have playgrounds, and the place for playgrounds is where they can be easily reached by the largest number of children. Since the same is true of schoolhouses and since work, study and play must go together in proper proportions in the education of every child, schoolgrounds and playgrounds should for the most part be identical. When erecting a building to cost $500,000, $25,000 is certainly not too much to invest in a site for the building and the necessary additional land for lawn, playgrounds; athletic field and school gardens. This is only 5% of the total cost.

2. Acquiring the Sites.

The board is therefore urged to get options on as large a plot as this amount will buy and do it as quietly as possible through trusted agents, before owners get wind of their intentions and boost the price. If, however, any price-boosting should be attempted it would be well to pick the plot, have a fair board of appraisers determine a just price, offer this price, and if it be not accepted, begin condemnation proceedings at once.

A similar site should be acquired for the west side school No. 12 and for the east side school No. 13 if there is any way in which it can be done legally. It will be poor business policy indeed to wait to buy these sites until the need for them is immediate and urgent. Plots that would be suitable and are now vacant land will, in all probability, be built on by that time and the board will then have to condemn and pay for houses that will be a dead loss and entail a great expense. If there is no legal way in which the board can acquire such land then an attempt should be made to get some wealthy and public-spirited citizen to buy the chosen plots and hold them for the board, until it can legally purchase them, at cost plus interest and taxes. No philanthropist could find a better way in which to help the city do a big thing for its children than to buy for the school board these three plots of land —as large plots as possible, and allow them to be used in the meantime as public playgrounds to be maintained by a suitable association formed for the purpose. When the time came for the board to buy, the philanthropist would have his capital back with interest plus tax payments, and would be making the city a present only of the unearned increment in the land value, an increment which the city itself will have created, and which therefore everybody should rejoice to have returned to it in such fair and generous fashion.

1. Washington School. This building was once abandoned and for very good reasons, but has been pressed into service to meet congested conditions. The lot is utterly unsuitable for school purposes. Heavy interurban cars pass frequently near the left side and also near the front of the buliding, which also overlooks a lumber yard and railway freight house. There are blast furnaces with their noisy blowing engines on the left, and the railway trains are passing and endlessly by its right and rear. It is choked and begrimed with smoke and dust. There are cracks in the walls everywhere, among them a very bad crack in the rear which looks dangerous. It is and always was as bad a fire trap as the notorious Collinwood building.

The lighting in all the rooms is grossly inadequate, being far below the standards required by state law.

The blackboards are inadequate in amount or in unfit condition for use in every room.

The toilet facilities are inadequate.

The third floor of the building is used by lodges and societies often during the daytime. It is dirty and poorly cared for, and these conditions add to the other annoyances.

This building unquestionably should be abandoned at the end of this school year, and should never be used for school purposes again. Any money spent in fixing it up will be worse than thrown away.

The school board could probably get a very good price for this property. In my opinion, they should sell it at the best price they can get, and use the money to buy sites for the new buildings, one of which I have shown will be needed immediately and the other two ultimately. The price which I believe they can get would buy the three sites wanted, erect the shop addition to McKinley high school, and go a long way toward buying all the equipment for the new east side school. I am not sure that it would not go farther than that.

I have learned that an influential body of citizens oppose the selling of this building, urging that the board keep it for a playground. I cannot see how the board can do this consistently with the functions for which it is created by the state. The board should not maintain one playground with capital that will buy three, when that one has no connection with a school building to be used immediately or in the future. If the city wants the Washington school lot for a playground and can afford to own it for that use, let the city buy it or let some generous person buy it and present it to the city.

It seems to me that for the board of education to retain this plot would obviously be unfair, since they could invest the capital involved to so much more advantage to all the children of the city. I therefore recommend that the board have this plot appraised by a fair and just board of competent experts, some of whom are not in any way interested in Niles real estate, and offered for sale at the highest bid above the appraisement. If widely advertised and sold in this way it ought to bring a very good price.

2. Monroe School. This school has four rooms and corridors so designed as to form half of an 8-room building. There is space on the lot for an addition to complete the building; but such an addition would in my opinion be a very bad investment; because the building is situated so near the railway tracks that during the frequent passages of trains the work of classes on that side of the building has to be stopped. Furthermore the character of the "loop" district where this building is located is such that its destiny as a residence district is very uncertain. It looks likely to become an area consisting of lumber yards, small factories and railroad switches, in which case it obviously would be bad business policy to invest money in buildings or additions for this district. In my judgment it will be better not to add to this building, but to wait and see what is going to happen. In the mean time if more rooms should be urgently needed here, which I do not think likely, a few good portable buildings can be placed on the lot on the side opposite that on which the railroad is.

The rooms of this building are dingy and need redecorating and many of the window shades are worn out, but the rooms in themselves are otherwise unobjectionable.

The worn out shades should be replaced by the tough semi-transparent adjustable school shades of the Draper type; and the walls should be repainted with a bright daffodil or light brown tone.

The toilets are none too clean, and should be kept cleaner, but otherwise are satisfactory.

3. Jefferson building. The rooms in this building are fairly well designed and well lighted. Two basement rooms have been pressed into service, which are too small for the number seated in them. Their use is justified in the emergency of the present year; but their use as classrooms should be discontinued as soon as possible.

The toilet facilities are satisfactory in quality but short in quantity. They are sufficient to provide according to Ohio legal standards for 350 pupils, while there are 450 pupils enrolled.

The building needs redecorating; and it needs more artificial lights distributed more efficiently. The number, power and distribution of artificial lights for school rooms should in every case be figured out by an illuminating expert before installing them.

This building has an adequate lot and is so constructed that an addition can be built on to it when necessary. When this addition is projected it should be planned to include an auditorium, gymnasium and laboratories for a complete nine grade school as recommended in the second chapter of this report.

4. Lincoln Building. This building is badly in need of redecorating. Many of the walls are badly cracked and need pointing up; and the old paint is scaling off in many places. The paint used is for the most part a glaring, crude and unpleasant green. A flat oil wall color—daffodil yellow or a light soft tone of brown should be used here, as has been recommended for all buildings.

5. Jackson Building. This building has 8 rooms and cannot be added to. It is built almost up to the sidewalk so the front rooms are exposed to the noise and dust of traffic. Like many

133623

buildings of its time in other cities, it is too small to be efficient, is badly located, is on too small a lot, and is not well designed. Under present circumstances however it is worth keeping in good repair, and should render fair service for a number of years to come.

6. Grant School. This two-room building is so poorly designed that it is nearly worthless for formal school work, though it will answer fairly for kindergarten and first grade. The light comes from three sides, giving rise to cross shadows which are very bad for the eyes. If the blinds are drawn on the right side to remedy this, then there will not be enough light. There is no way to correct this condition.

I advise that this building be abandoned as soon as feasible— next year if it can be—or used only as a kindergarten.

Kindergartens should be started in Niles and this would be a good place to start one next year. I recommend this proposal for serious consideration. If so used the rooms should be redecorated, made artistic and home like, and fitted out with kindergarten materials and storage cabinets in which to keep them.

The blackboards now in use are of the plaster variety and very poor.

After the present state of congestion has been effectively relieved I believe that this building and lot should be abandoned and sold.

The other buildings require no further comment.

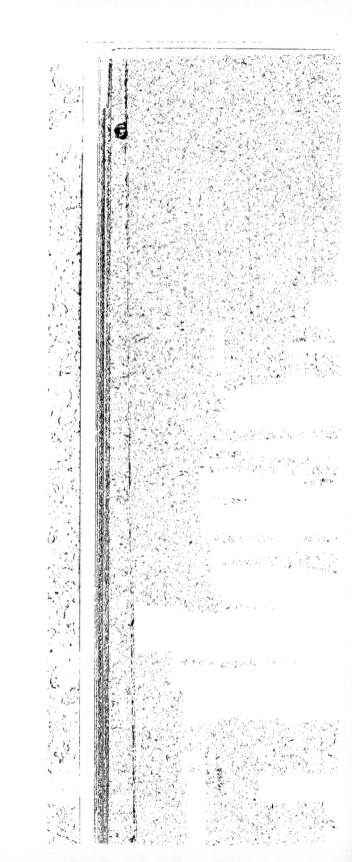

TABLE IA

SUMMARY OF TABLE I BY BUILDINGS SHOWING WHERE THE CONGESTION IS IN GRADES. I—VI.

1 Name of Building	2 Number on Map	3 Legal Number of Pupils	4 Number of Pupils Enrolled	5 Pupils in Excess of Legal Number	6 Number of Seats	7 Seats in Excess of Legal Number	8 Pupils in Excess of Seats	9 Second Platoon	10 Net Pupils in Excess of Legal Numbers	11 Net Seats in Excess of Legal Number	12 Net Pupils in Excess of Seats
Jefferson	1	44	446	—12 34 (6 Rms.)	443	—12 31 (5 Rms.)	—3 6 (2 Rms.)		22	19	3
Lincoln	2	373	356	—21 5 (3 Rms.) 4	363	—15 17 (3 Rms.)	—34 2	42	—30	2	35
Jackson	3	369	339	—35 5 (2 Rms.)	371	—12 2 (1 Rm.)	—10 3 (1 Rm.)				
Garfield	4	185	198	—6 59 (2 Rms.)	233	—16 64 (1 Rm.)	—35		13	48	—35
Monroe	5	180	142	—35	174	—10 4 (1 Rm.)	—32		—38	—6	—32
Harrison	6	137	137	—7 7 (2 Rms.)	164	27 (4 Rms.)	—27		0	27	—27
Grant	7	112	112	—27	88	—24	—3	46	—27	—24	43
The Seven Buildings Combined		1780	1703	—186 109	1836	—89 145	—144 11	88	—112 35	96	—126
Washington	8	134	118	—16	130	—4	—12		—16	—4	—12
McKinley H. S.	9		298								
Roosevelt	10	306	Proposed 336								30

TABLE II.

T BY GRADES AND BUILDINGS, SHOWING FOR ALL ELEMENTARY GRADES, THE INCREASES AND PERCENTAGE INCREASES FROM 1915 TO 1920

	Grade I			Grade II			Grade III			Grade IV			Grade V			Grade VI			Grade VII			Grade VIII			All Grades		
	1915	1920	In-crease	1915	1920	In-crease	1915	1920	In-crease	1915	1920	In-crease	1915	1920	In-crease	1915	1920	In-crease	1915	1920	In-crease	1915	1920	In-crease	1915	1920	In-crease
1	40	86	46	41	93	52	31	45	14	40	45	5	41	89	48	72	86	14	36		—36				301	444	143
2	53	102	49	55	74	19	49	48	—1	45	65	20	46	51	5	34	58	24	17		—17				299	398	99
3	56	89	33	47	26	—21	48	59	11	50	42	—8	44	43	—1	64	80	16	17		—17				326	339	13
4	32	47	15	31	37	6	23	22	—1	18	34	16	21	27	6	19	34	15	20		—20				164	201	37
5	42	71	29	42		—42	41	34	—7	37	38	1													162	143	—19
6		37	37		19	19		22	22		22	22		14	14		18	18		8	8				0	140	140
7		42	42		43	43		46	46												39	39				0	131	131
											37	37								39			40	40	0	116	116
																			62	156	94	118	142	24	180	298	118
	223	474	251	216	292	76	192	276	84	190	283	93	152	224	72	189	276	87	152	203	51	118	182	64	1432	2210	778
crease			112.6			35.2			44.7			48.9			47.4			46.0			33.6			154.3			154.3

TABLE II-A.

CALCULATION OF INCREASE OF SCHOOL POPULATION.

Grade	Enrolment 1915	1920	Increase 5 yrs.	% Increase
I -------------------	223	474	251	112.6
II -------------------	216	292	76	35.2
III -------------------	192	276	84	44.7
IV -------------------	190	283	93	48.9
V -------------------	152	224	72	47.4
VI -------------------	189	276	87	46.0
I_VI combined -----------	1162	1825	663	57
VII -------------------	152	203	51	33.6
VIII -------------------	118	182	64	54 2
VII_VIII combined -----------	270	385	115	42.6
I_VIII combined -----------	1432	2210	778	54.3
IX -------------------	137	133	—4	—3
X -------------------	82	114	32	39
XI -------------------	57	83	26	46
XII -------------------	40	70	30	75
IX-XII combined -----------	316	400	84	27
I-XII combined -----------	1748	2610	862	49

$2210 \times .54 = 1193$, the estimated increase by 1925, Grades I-VIII.
$400 \times .27 = 108$, the estimated increase by 1925, High School.

Total increase 1301

$1301 \div 5 = 260+$ estimated annual increase, all grades.
$1193 \div 5 = 239-$ estimated annual increase, grades I-VIII.
$108 \div 5 = 21-$ estimated annual increase, grades IX-XII.

TABLE III.

ANALYSIS OF DATA FROM TABLES I AND II FOR DETERMINING
THE NUMBER OF PUPILS FOR WHOM ADDITIONAL BUILDING
CAPACITY MUST BE PROVIDED

1 BUILDINGS	2 Total capacity on basis of legal air space	3 Less capacity unfit for other reasons	4 Net capacity available according to standards	5 Number of pupils enrolled 1921	6 Excess space	7 Excess Pupils
Jefferson	424	64	360	446	--	86
Lincoln	373	--	373	397	--	24
Garfield	204	19	185	198	--	13
Jackson	369	--	369	339	30	--
Monroe	180	---	180	142	38	--
Harrison	137	---	137	137	--	--
Washington	134	134	---	118	--	118
Grant	112	112	---	131	--	131
Elementary buildings combined	1933	329	1604	1908	68	372
McKinley (capacity estimated)			663	698	--	35
Total present capacity (net)			2267	2606	68	407
Roosevelt, Sept. 1921			306	----	306	---
Garfield Addition, 1921			228	----	228	---
Total net capacity present and projected			2801		602	407
Estimated increase enrolment by 1925-6				1301		1301
Additional pupil capacity required 1925			1106	----	602	1708
Estimated Total 1925-6			3907	3907		

Number of rooms required on basis of 40 pupils per room $\dfrac{1106}{40} = 28$

Number of rooms required on basis of 35 pupils per room $\dfrac{1106}{35} = 32$

TABLE IV.

DISTRIBUTION OF THE NILES SCHOOL ENROLMENT ACCORDING TO
SCHOOLS AND SECTIONS OF THE CITY, AS REVEALED
BY COUNT OF THE PIN-MAPS.

Section of City	1A	1B	2A	2B	3	Loop	4	Total
Senior High (Grades IX-XII)	30	105	40	110	20	4	18	327*
Junior High (grades VII-VIII)	27	74	49	92	49	47	55	393
Jefferson _____	0	0	3	28	312	103	0	446
Lincoln _____	6	0	88	219	36	46	0	395
Jackson _____	48	255	5	2	0	4	0	314
Garfield _____	0	3	0	0	1	1	183	188
Monroe _____	0	0	0	0	21	118	0	139
Grant. _____								170
Washington (4th grade) (Old Central) _____								37
Harrison _____								140
	111	437	185	451	439	323	256	2549

* Senior High School registration incomplete. The total is 400.

TABLE V.

INCREASE IN ENROLMENT, GRADES VII-XII, 1915-1920.

1	2	3	4	5	6	7	8
Grade	Year 1915	Year 1920	Increase	Percent Increase	In McKinley Building	In Washington Building	In Harrison Building
XII _____	40	70	30	75.0	70	--	--
XI _____	57	83	26	45.6	83	--	--
X _____	82	114	32	39.0	114	--	--
IX _____	137	133	—4	—2.9	133	--	--
Total IX-XII ____	316	400	84	26.6	400	--	--
VIII _____	118	182	64	54.2	142	40	--
VII _____	152	203	51	33.6	156	39	8
Total VII-VIII __	270	385	115	42.6	298	79	
Total VII-XII ____	586	785	199	34.0	698	79	8

TABLE VI.

CALCULATION OF WORKING CAPACITY OF McKINLEY HIGH SCHOOL BUILDING.

Note.—The calculation is based on the following assumptions: (1) That the average size of class section is 25 pupils. (2) That the average pupil will spend 1-3 of his time in study hall gymnasium and 2-3 in class rooms and special rooms. (3) That as a result of (2) the maximum enrolment theoretically can be 1-3 greater than the combined class room and special room capacity. (4) That an allowance of 15% must be deducted from the maximum theoretical capacity on account of pupils taking extra subjects, on account of the existence of small classes in certain subjects and on account of numerous other unavoidable contingencies in adjusting classes to rooms and time schedule.

Kinds of Rooms	Number of such rooms	Pupils per room	Capacity
Medium sized classrooms _____	14	25	350
Small classrooms _____	3	25	75
Cooking, Chemistry, Typing _____	3	20	60
Sewing, Commercial, Physics _____	4	25	100
Combined _____	24		585
Plus 1-3 in Study Hall and Gym. _____			195
Total capacity, theoretical _____			780
Less contingent allowance 15% _____			117
Net capacity, practical _____			663
Study Halls _____	2	108 & 80	182
Gymnasium _____	1	40	40
Combined _____	3		222
Required (theoretical) 1-3 of 780 _____			260
Theoretical shortage _____			38
Auditorium _____	1	800	800

TABLE VII.

CALCULATION AND ESTIMATE FOR ENROLMENT, GRADES VII-XII FOR SEPTEMBER 1921.

Section A.

Present enrolment Grades IX-XII --------------------		400
VIII promoted to IX (McKinley) ---------------------		142
VIII promoted to IX (Washington) ------------------		40
From Weathersfield Township ----------------------		30
From Parochial Schools (Est.) ---------------------		20
Total, Grades IX-XII ------------------------------		632
Less loss by graduation ---------------------------	70	
Less loss by estimated eliminations ----------------	30	100
Net probable enrolment IX-XII ---------------------		532
VI promoted to VII (see Section D, below) ---------		238
VII promoted to VIII (see Section D below) --------		184
Total probable enrolment VII-XII ------------------		954
Excess over present total of 777 ------------------		177

Section B.

Grade	1915	1920	Gain	% gain 5 years	Average % gain, 1 year
VI ------------------	189	276	87	46	9.2
VII ------------------	152	203	51	33.6	6.7
VIII ------------------	118	182	64	54.2	10.8

Section C.

Grade	1915 Enrolment	1915 loss	1916 % loss	1920 Enrolment	1921 Loss	1921 % loss	Average % loss
VI -------------	189	--	---	276	--	---	---
VII ------------	152	37	19.6	203	73	26.4	23.0
VIII -----------	118	34	22.4	182	21	10.3	16.3

Section D.

1920 Grade	Loss	Gain	Net loss	1920 enrolment	Net loss	Estimated enrolment '21	1921 Grade
VI ------	23.0%	9.2%	13.8%	276 ·	38	238	VII
VII -----	16.3%	6.7%	9.6%	203	19	184	VIII

Lightning Source UK Ltd.
Milton Keynes UK
UKHW012330061118
331891UK00010B/976/P